The Quantum Leap

The Quantum Leap

UNRAVELING THE MYSTERIES OF REALITY

Anurag

Anurag Anurag

Contents

1

Quantum Foundations

In the opening chapter of "The Quantum Leap," we embark on a journey into the fundamental principles of quantum mechanics. Imagine a world where particles behave both as waves and particles simultaneously, a concept known as wave-particle duality. The famous double-slit experiment serves as our guide, demonstrating how particles, such as electrons, can exhibit wave-like behavior when not observed, yet collapse into particles when observed.

Schrödinger's cat illustrates another bizarre phenomenon of quantum mechanics: superposition. In this thought experiment, a cat enclosed in a box is simultaneously alive and dead until observed, reflecting the concept that quantum particles can exist in multiple states at once. This notion challenges our classical intuition but lies at the heart of quantum theory.

Quantum tunneling, exemplified by the phenomenon of particles passing through energy barriers seemingly forbidden by classical physics, further stretches our understanding of reality. Imagine a scenario where an electron "magically" tunnels through a potential barrier, defying the laws of classical physics. This quantum behavior has practical applications in various fields, from electronics to nuclear fusion.

Heisenberg's uncertainty principle introduces yet another layer of complexity to quantum mechanics. This principle states that the more precisely we know a particle's position, the less precisely we can know its momentum, and vice versa. Consider an electron's position and velocity —attempting to measure one with absolute certainty introduces uncertainty into the measurement of the other, fundamentally altering our perception of reality.

Bell's theorem and the EPR paradox reveal the mysterious interconnectedness of quantum particles, even when separated by vast distances. Imagine two entangled particles whose properties remain correlated regardless of the distance between them. This non-local connection challenges our classical understanding of locality and underscores the enigmatic nature of quantum entanglement.

The chapter also explores practical applications of quantum mechanics, such as quantum cryptography, which utilizes the principles of entanglement to secure communication channels. Imagine encoding information into entangled particles, ensuring that any eavesdropping attempt disrupts the entanglement, thus alerting the sender and preserving the integrity of the communication.

Quantum computing represents another groundbreaking application of quantum mechanics, promising to revolutionize computation by harnessing the power of superposition and entanglement. Imagine a computer capable of performing vast calculations simultaneously, thanks to quantum bits or qubits existing in multiple states at once. Such a quantum computer could solve complex problems exponentially faster than classical computers.

Quantum teleportation pushes the boundaries of our imagination even further, enabling the transfer of quantum information from one location to another without physical transmission. Imagine encoding the state of a particle onto an entangled pair, then transmitting this information instantaneously to a distant location, effectively "teleporting" the particle's state.

Finally, quantum biology explores the role of quantum effects in biological processes, challenging the traditional view of biology as solely governed by classical physics. Imagine photosynthesis, where quantum coherence enables efficient energy transfer in plants, inspiring researchers to harness quantum principles for novel technologies.

Through these examples and insights, "The Quantum Leap" sets the stage for a deeper exploration of quantum mechanics and its profound implications for our understanding of reality.

<h1 align="center">2</h1>

: Quantum Entanglement

In this chapter, we delve into the mysterious phenomenon of quantum entanglement, where particles become intrinsically connected in ways that defy classical intuition. Picture two particles, such as photons, generated in an entangled state, their properties instantly correlated regardless of the distance between them. This instantaneous correlation, famously described by Einstein as "spooky action at a distance," challenges our understanding of causality and locality.

Bell's inequality provides a rigorous test of quantum entanglement, revealing that no local hidden variable theory can reproduce all the predictions of quantum mechanics. Imagine a series of experiments confirming the violation of Bell's inequality, demonstrating the non-classical nature of entangled particles and the limitations of local realism.

Aspect's experiments further confirm the reality of quantum entanglement, ruling out alternative explanations and solidifying entanglement as a fundamental feature of quantum mechanics. Through meticulous measurements and careful analysis, researchers have confirmed that entangled particles do indeed exhibit correlated behaviors, even when separated by vast distances.

Entanglement swapping allows us to extend quantum connections beyond pairs of directly entangled particles, enabling the creation of entangled states between particles that have never interacted directly. Imagine a scenario where entangled photons A and B interact with separate photons C and D, resulting in entangled states between photons A and D, as well as B and C. This phenomenon demonstrates the remarkable flexibility of entanglement and its potential applications in quantum communication and computing.

Quantum teleportation offers a practical demonstration of entanglement's power, allowing the transfer of quantum information from one location to another without physical transmission. Imagine encoding the quantum state of a particle onto an entangled pair, then using classical communication to transmit information about the original particle's state. At the receiving end, the state of a third particle is transformed into an exact replica of the original, demonstrating the transfer of quantum information through entanglement.

Quantum networks represent the next frontier in entanglement-based communication systems, enabling secure and efficient transmission of quantum information over long distances. Imagine a global network of entangled particles, forming the backbone of a quantum internet capable of transmitting information instantaneously and securely across the globe. Such a network could revolutionize fields ranging from cryptography to distributed computing.

Quantum entanglement finds applications in diverse fields, from particle physics to cosmology, offering insights into the fundamental nature of reality and the interconnectedness of the universe. Imagine entangled particles playing a role in phenomena such as black hole evaporation or the early universe, providing clues to some of the most profound questions in physics.

In everyday life, quantum entanglement has practical implications, from quantum cryptography to quantum teleportation, promising to revolutionize communication, computation, and information processing. Imagine a future where quantum technologies harness the power of entanglement to create secure communication channels, ultra-fast computers, and novel methods of information transfer.

Through these examples and insights, "The Quantum Leap" illuminates the mysterious world of quantum entanglement, challenging our classical intuitions and opening new avenues for exploration and discovery in the quest to understand the nature of reality.

3

Quantum Computing

In this chapter, we explore the revolutionary potential of quantum computing, a paradigm-shifting technology poised to transform the landscape of computation. Imagine a computer that harnesses the principles of superposition and entanglement to perform calculations exponentially faster than classical computers. This is the promise of quantum computing, a field that holds the key to unlocking unprecedented computational power and solving complex problems that are currently beyond the reach of classical algorithms.

At the heart of quantum computing lies the quantum bit, or qubit, the fundamental unit of quantum information. Unlike classical bits, which can only exist in a state of 0 or 1, qubits can exist in a superposition of both states simultaneously, enabling quantum computers to perform vast numbers of calculations in parallel.

Quantum algorithms leverage the unique properties of qubits to solve computational problems more efficiently than classical algorithms. One example is Shor's algorithm, which factors large numbers exponentially faster than the best-known classical algorithms. Imagine a future where quantum computers render current encryption methods obsolete, posing both opportunities and challenges for cybersecurity and information security.

Another example is Grover's algorithm, which can search an unsorted database quadratically faster than classical algorithms. Imagine a scenario where quantum computers revolutionize data search and optimization, offering unprecedented speed and efficiency in finding solutions to complex problems.

Despite these promising advancements, quantum computing faces significant technical challenges, including decoherence and error correction. Decoherence occurs when qubits interact with their environment, causing them to lose their quantum properties and behave classically. Error correction techniques, such as quantum error correction codes, aim to mitigate these errors and preserve the integrity of quantum computations.

Practical quantum computers are still in the early stages of development, with current devices limited to a small number of qubits and rudimentary operations. However, rapid progress is being made in both academia and industry, with companies investing heavily in quantum hardware and software development.

Quantum supremacy, the milestone at which a quantum computer can outperform the best classical computers for a specific task, represents a significant benchmark in the field of quantum computing. Imagine a quantum computer demonstrating supremacy by solving a problem that is intractable for classical computers, heralding a new era of quantum supremacy.

The potential applications of quantum computing are vast and varied, spanning fields such as cryptography, drug discovery, materials science, and artificial intelligence. Imagine a future where quantum computers revolutionize drug development by simulating molecular structures with unprecedented accuracy, leading to the discovery of new drugs and treatments for a wide range of diseases.

Through ongoing research and innovation, quantum computing promises to unlock new frontiers of scientific discovery and technological advancement, paving the way for a future limited only by the bounds of our imagination.

4

Quantum Teleportation

In this chapter, we delve into the mind-bending phenomenon of quantum teleportation, a concept that challenges our notions of space, time, and information transfer. Imagine a scenario where the quantum state of a particle is transferred from one location to another instantaneously, without traversing the physical space between them. This is the essence of quantum teleportation, a process that relies on the principles of quantum entanglement and classical communication to transmit quantum information.

Quantum teleportation begins with the creation of an entangled pair of particles, typically photons, which share a correlated state regardless of the distance between them. Imagine encoding the quantum state of a third particle onto one half of the entangled pair, effectively entangling it with the other particle. This process transfers the quantum information from the original particle to the entangled pair, setting the stage for teleportation.

Next, imagine performing a series of measurements on the entangled pair and the particle whose state is to be teleported. These measurements yield classical information that is communicated to the receiving end via classical communication channels. Based on these measurements, the quantum state of the original particle can be reconstructed at the receiving end, effectively teleporting its state from one location to another.

Quantum teleportation has been experimentally demonstrated with various quantum systems, including photons, atoms, and ions. Imagine a laboratory setup where scientists successfully teleport the quantum state of photons over long distances, laying the groundwork for practical applications such as secure communication and quantum networking.

One of the most promising applications of quantum teleportation is in the field of quantum communication, where it enables the secure transmission of quantum information over long distances. Imagine encoding sensitive information onto quantum states and teleporting them between distant locations, safe from eavesdropping or interception due to the inherent security of quantum mechanics.

Quantum teleportation also plays a crucial role in quantum computing, where it enables the transfer of quantum information between different components of a quantum computer. Imagine a future where quantum computers leverage teleportation to perform distributed computations across a network of interconnected quantum processors, unlocking unprecedented computational power and scalability.

Beyond communication and computing, quantum teleportation holds potential applications in fields such as quantum cryptography, quantum metrology, and quantum sensing. Imagine using teleportation to synchronize clocks with unprecedented precision or to detect gravitational waves with enhanced sensitivity, pushing the boundaries of scientific exploration and discovery.

While quantum teleportation remains a nascent technology with many technical challenges to overcome, its potential for revolutionizing communication, computing, and sensing is vast and exciting. Through continued research and innovation, we may one day realize the full potential of quantum teleportation and unlock its transformative capabilities for the benefit of society.

5

Quantum Cryptography

In this chapter, we explore the fascinating world of quantum cryptography, a field that harnesses the principles of quantum mechanics to secure communication channels against eavesdropping and interception. Imagine a scenario where information is encoded onto individual quantum particles, such as photons, and transmitted between parties using quantum protocols that exploit the inherent properties of quantum mechanics for secure communication.

The foundation of quantum cryptography lies in the principle of quantum indeterminacy, which states that measuring a quantum system disturbs its state, making it impossible for an eavesdropper to intercept the communication without being detected. Imagine encoding information onto the polarization states of photons and transmitting them between parties using quantum key distribution protocols that rely on the properties of entanglement and superposition to ensure the security of the communication channel.

One of the most well-known quantum cryptographic protocols is the BB84 protocol, proposed by Charles Bennett and Gilles Brassard in 1984. Imagine a scenario where Alice wishes to communicate securely with Bob over an insecure channel. By encoding her message onto randomly chosen quantum states and sending them to Bob, Alice can establish a secret key with Bob that is secure against eavesdropping attempts.

Quantum key distribution (QKD) protocols enable the generation of a secret key between two parties that can be used to encrypt and decrypt messages securely. Imagine Alice and Bob performing a QKD protocol to generate a shared secret key, which they can then use to encrypt their communication using classical encryption algorithms such as AES or RSA, ensuring the confidentiality and integrity of their messages.

Quantum cryptography offers several advantages over classical cryptographic techniques, including unconditional security and the ability to detect eavesdropping attempts with high probability. Imagine an eavesdropper, Eve, attempting to intercept the communication between Alice and Bob. Due to the principles of quantum mechanics, any attempt by Eve to measure the quantum states of the photons will disturb their states, alerting Alice and Bob to the presence of an eavesdropper.

Quantum cryptography has practical applications in secure communication channels, financial transactions, and data privacy protection. Imagine a future where quantum cryptographic protocols are integrated into existing communication networks, ensuring the security and integrity of sensitive information exchanged between parties.

While quantum cryptography holds great promise for enhancing security in the digital age, challenges remain in the practical implementation of quantum cryptographic systems, including the development of robust quantum hardware and the integration of quantum protocols into existing communication infrastructure. Through continued research and innovation, quantum cryptography has the potential to revolutionize the way we secure communication channels and protect sensitive information in an increasingly interconnected world.

6
꩜

Quantum Biology

In this chapter, we explore the fascinating intersection of quantum mechanics and biology, a field known as quantum biology. Quantum biology investigates how quantum phenomena, such as superposition, entanglement, and coherence, influence biological processes at the molecular and cellular levels. Imagine a world where quantum effects play a crucial role in the fundamental processes of life, from photosynthesis to DNA replication, challenging our traditional understanding of biology.

Photosynthesis serves as one of the most striking examples of quantum effects in biological systems. Imagine a scenario where quantum coherence enables efficient energy transfer in photosynthetic complexes, allowing plants to harvest sunlight with remarkable efficiency. By exploiting quantum coherence, plants are able to navigate complex energy landscapes and transfer energy across large distances with minimal loss, leading to the development of novel technologies for renewable energy and artificial photosynthesis.

Another example of quantum biology is the phenomenon of quantum tunneling in enzyme-catalyzed reactions. Imagine a scenario where enzymes facilitate chemical reactions by lowering the energy barrier that molecules must overcome to react. Quantum tunneling allows particles to tunnel through energy barriers that would be insurmountable according to classical physics, enabling enzymatic reactions to proceed at rates that would otherwise be impossible.

The role of quantum coherence in avian navigation provides another intriguing example of quantum biology. Imagine a scenario where birds use quantum coherence to sense the Earth's magnetic field and navigate during migration. By exploiting quantum effects in specialized molecules called cryptochromes, birds are able to detect subtle variations in the Earth's magnetic field and orient themselves accordingly, guiding their migratory journeys with remarkable precision.

Quantum biology also extends to the field of neuroscience, where quantum phenomena may play a role in the mechanisms of consciousness and cognition. Imagine a scenario where quantum coherence and entanglement in neural networks give rise to emergent properties such as consciousness and subjective experience. While the exact nature of the relationship between quantum mechanics and consciousness remains speculative, ongoing research in this area holds the potential to deepen our understanding of the mind-brain relationship.

Despite the exciting discoveries in quantum biology, many questions remain unanswered, and the field is still in its infancy. Challenges such as decoherence, the process by which quantum systems interact with their environment and lose their quantum properties, pose significant obstacles to the study of quantum effects in biological systems.

However, the potential applications of quantum biology are vast, ranging from novel therapies for disease to the development of bio-inspired technologies. Imagine a future where insights from quantum biology lead to the design of quantum-inspired drugs that target disease at the molecular level or the development of quantum-inspired sensors that detect biomarkers with unprecedented sensitivity.

Through interdisciplinary collaboration and innovative research, quantum biology offers a new lens through which to explore the mysteries of life and the universe, bridging the gap between the quantum world and the biological realm.

7

Quantum Cosmology

In this chapter, we embark on a journey to explore the profound implications of quantum mechanics for our understanding of the cosmos, a field known as quantum cosmology. Imagine a universe governed by both quantum mechanics and gravity, where the laws of physics break down at the smallest scales and the fabric of spacetime itself is subject to quantum fluctuations.

At the heart of quantum cosmology lies the quest for a theory of quantum gravity, a framework that reconciles the principles of quantum mechanics with the theory of general relativity. Imagine a scenario where quantum fluctuations in the fabric of spacetime give rise to the birth of the universe itself, leading to the formation of galaxies, stars, and planets over billions of years.

One of the most intriguing questions in quantum cosmology is the nature of the Big Bang, the event that marks the beginning of our universe. Imagine a scenario where the universe emerges from a primordial state of quantum fluctuations, with space and time undergoing rapid expansion in the early moments of the Big Bang. By probing the cosmic microwave background radiation, scientists aim to uncover clues about the universe's earliest moments and test theories of quantum cosmology.

The concept of quantum entanglement also plays a role in cosmology, offering insights into the interconnectedness of the universe on the largest scales. Imagine a scenario where distant regions of the cosmos are entangled, their properties correlated in ways that defy classical intuition. By studying the cosmic web of galaxies and the distribution of matter in the universe, astronomers hope to uncover evidence of quantum entanglement on cosmic scales.

Another intriguing concept in quantum cosmology is the multiverse hypothesis, which posits the existence of multiple universes parallel to our own. Imagine a scenario where quantum fluctuations give rise to the creation of new universes, each with its own laws of physics and properties. By exploring the implications of the multiverse hypothesis, physicists aim to answer fundamental questions about the nature of reality and the existence of other universes beyond our own.

Quantum cosmology also intersects with the study of black holes, the enigmatic objects formed from the collapse of massive stars. Imagine a scenario where the quantum nature of black holes leads to the resolution of the black hole information paradox, a puzzle that has perplexed physicists for decades. By applying the principles of quantum mechanics to black hole physics, scientists aim to uncover the secrets of these cosmic phenomena and shed light on the fundamental nature of spacetime and gravity.

While many questions remain unanswered, quantum cosmology offers a tantalizing glimpse into the deepest mysteries of the cosmos, from the origin of the universe to the nature of black holes and the existence of parallel universes. Through theoretical exploration, observational evidence, and experimental verification, quantum cosmology continues to push the boundaries of human knowledge and inspire wonder and awe at the vastness and complexity of the universe.

8

Quantum Consciousness

In this chapter, we delve into the intriguing intersection of quantum mechanics and consciousness, exploring the possibility that quantum phenomena may play a role in the mysteries of the mind. Imagine a scenario where the enigmatic nature of quantum mechanics offers insights into the nature of consciousness, challenging our traditional views of the mind-brain relationship and opening new avenues for understanding human cognition and subjective experience.

One of the most tantalizing questions in quantum consciousness is whether quantum effects play a role in the emergence of consciousness itself. Imagine a scenario where the brain's neural networks exhibit quantum properties such as superposition and entanglement, leading to the emergence of consciousness as a result of quantum processes occurring at the microscopic level. While speculative, this hypothesis suggests a profound connection between the quantum world and the subjective experience of consciousness.

The phenomenon of quantum superposition offers a potential explanation for the complexity and flexibility of human cognition. Imagine a scenario where neural networks exploit quantum superposition to explore multiple cognitive states simultaneously, enabling rapid and flexible decision-making in response to changing environmental conditions. By harnessing the principles of quantum mechanics, the brain may achieve computational feats that are beyond the capabilities of classical computers.

Another intriguing concept in quantum consciousness is the role of quantum coherence in the integration of information across different brain regions. Imagine a scenario where quantum coherence enables the synchronization of neural activity across the brain, facilitating the integration of sensory information, memory recall, and higher-order cognitive functions. By maintaining coherence over large spatial and temporal scales, the brain may achieve the remarkable feat of unified conscious experience.

Quantum entanglement offers yet another avenue for exploring the mysteries of consciousness. Imagine a scenario where entangled particles within the brain establish non-local connections between different brain regions, enabling the rapid exchange of information and the emergence of coherent patterns of neural activity. By exploiting entanglement, the brain may achieve a level of interconnectedness and integration that is essential for conscious experience.

While the hypothesis of quantum consciousness remains speculative and controversial, ongoing research in this area holds the potential to deepen our understanding of the mind-brain relationship and the nature of consciousness itself. By bridging the gap between quantum mechanics and neuroscience, quantum consciousness offers a new framework for exploring the mysteries of the human mind and unlocking the secrets of subjective experience.

Through interdisciplinary collaboration and innovative research, quantum consciousness continues to push the boundaries of scientific inquiry and challenge our assumptions about the nature of reality and the human experience.

9

Quantum Ethics

In this chapter, we explore the implications of quantum mechanics for the field of ethics, examining how the principles of quantum mechanics may inform our understanding of morality and decision-making. Imagine a scenario where the uncertainty and indeterminacy of quantum mechanics extend beyond the realm of particles and into the realm of human behavior, challenging traditional notions of moral responsibility and free will.

One of the central questions in quantum ethics is whether the uncertainty inherent in quantum mechanics has implications for human decision-making and moral judgment. Imagine a scenario where human choices are influenced by quantum randomness, leading to unpredictable outcomes and blurring the lines between free will and determinism. By examining the parallels between quantum uncertainty and moral ambiguity, we can gain new insights into the nature of ethical decision-making.

The concept of quantum entanglement offers another perspective on ethics, highlighting the interconnectedness and interdependence of human actions and their consequences. Imagine a scenario where the consequences of our actions are entangled with the choices of others, creating complex moral dilemmas and ethical responsibilities. By recognizing the interconnectedness of all beings, we can cultivate a sense of empathy and compassion that extends beyond individual interests to encompass the well-being of the entire quantum community.

Quantum superposition challenges traditional notions of moral absolutes and binary categories of right and wrong. Imagine a scenario where moral values exist in a state of superposition, simultaneously valid and invalid until observed and measured by human consciousness. By embracing the uncertainty and complexity of moral decision-making, we can move beyond rigid moral frameworks and cultivate a more nuanced and adaptive approach to ethics.

The phenomenon of quantum tunneling offers a metaphor for the possibility of moral transformation and personal growth. Imagine a scenario where individuals are able to overcome moral barriers and entrenched patterns of behavior through a process of quantum tunneling, transcending the limitations of past actions and opening up new possibilities for moral agency and ethical engagement. By harnessing the power of quantum tunneling, we can break free from moral inertia and catalyze positive change in ourselves and society.

While the concept of quantum ethics remains speculative and philosophical, it offers a thought-provoking framework for exploring the complexities of human morality and decision-making. By drawing parallels between quantum phenomena and ethical principles, we can deepen our understanding of the ethical implications of quantum mechanics and cultivate a more holistic and compassionate approach to ethics in an interconnected world.

Through interdisciplinary dialogue and ethical reflection, quantum ethics invites us to reconsider our assumptions about the nature of morality and embrace the uncertainty and complexity of ethical decision-making in a rapidly changing world.

10

Quantum Spirituality

In this final chapter, we embark on a journey to explore the intersection of quantum mechanics and spirituality, examining how the principles of quantum physics may offer insights into the nature of consciousness, the universe, and the human experience. Imagine a scenario where the mysteries of quantum mechanics inspire awe and wonder, inviting us to contemplate the profound interconnectedness of all things and the underlying unity of existence.

One of the central themes in quantum spirituality is the idea of non-locality, which suggests that particles can be instantaneously connected across vast distances. Imagine a scenario where this non-local interconnectedness extends beyond the realm of particles and into the realm of consciousness, suggesting that we are all interconnected in a vast web of existence. By recognizing our inherent connection to all beings and to the universe itself, we can cultivate a sense of spiritual unity and interconnectedness that transcends the boundaries of space and time.

The concept of quantum entanglement offers another perspective on spirituality, highlighting the idea of oneness and interdependence. Imagine a scenario where the entanglement of particles reflects a deeper cosmic unity, where the separation between self and other is illusory and all beings are part of a single, interconnected whole. By embracing the concept of entanglement, we can cultivate a sense of spiritual interconnectedness and compassion that extends beyond the individual ego to encompass the well-being of all sentient beings.

Quantum coherence offers a metaphor for spiritual harmony and alignment, suggesting that when our thoughts, emotions, and actions are in coherence, we experience a state of inner peace and harmony. Imagine a scenario where the coherence of our consciousness reflects the coherence of the quantum world, where our inner state of harmony is reflected in the harmony of the universe itself. By cultivating inner coherence through practices such as meditation, mindfulness, and self-reflection, we can align ourselves with the underlying order and harmony of the cosmos.

The phenomenon of quantum superposition challenges our conventional notions of reality and invites us to explore the realm of infinite possibility. Imagine a scenario where our consciousness exists in a state of superposition, simultaneously experiencing multiple states of being and infinite potentialities. By embracing the inherent uncertainty and openness of quantum superposition, we can cultivate a sense of spiritual openness and curiosity, allowing us to explore new dimensions of consciousness and experience.

While the concept of quantum spirituality remains speculative and philosophical, it offers a thought-provoking framework for exploring the mysteries of existence and our place in the universe. By drawing parallels between quantum phenomena and spiritual principles, we can deepen our understanding of the nature of reality and cultivate a more profound and holistic approach to spirituality in an interconnected world.

Through contemplation, reflection, and spiritual practice, quantum spirituality invites us to awaken to the profound mysteries of existence and embrace the inherent unity and interconnectedness of all things. In doing so, we may discover new depths of meaning, purpose, and fulfillment in our lives, and contribute to the emergence of a more compassionate, harmonious, and spiritually awakened world.